STEPHEN HAWKING
HIS LIFE AND LEGACY

BY EMILY SCHLESINGER

NONFICTION

Alaska's Iditarod
Children of the Holocaust
Cryptocurrency
Deadly Bites
Digital Worlds
Droids and Robots
Esports
Flight Squads

The Music Industry
Navajo Code Talkers
Olympic Games
Stephen Hawking
Superbugs
The White House
Working Dogs
World Cup Soccer

www.sdlback.com

Copyright © 2021 by Saddleback Educational Publishing
All rights reserved. No part of this book may be reproduced in any form or by any means, electronic or mechanical, including photocopying, recording, scanning, or by any information storage and retrieval system, without the written permission of the publisher. SADDLEBACK EDUCATIONAL PUBLISHING and any associated logos are trademarks and/or registered trademarks of Saddleback Educational Publishing.

Photo credits: page 2: Frederick M. Brown / Getty Images Entertainment via Getty Images; pages 6/7: Jemal Countess / Getty Images Entertainment via Getty Images; page 8: Hulton Archive / Getty Hulton Archive via Getty Images; pages 8/9: David Silverman / Getty Images News via Getty Images; pages 16/17: David Williams / The Image Bank via Getty Images; page 22: DESIREE MARTIN / AFP via Getty Images; page 27: MPI / Archive Photos via Getty Images; pages 28/29: Mirrorpix / Mirrorpix via Getty Images; page 33: Jack Taylor / Getty Images News via Getty Images; pages 34/35: The Asahi Shimbun / The Asahi Shimbun via Getty Images; page 39: Michelly Rall / Getty Images News via Getty Images; pages 40/41: Mirrorpix / Mirrorpix via Getty Images; pages 44/45: Jack Taylo / Getty Images News via Getty Images; page 47: Mike Flokis / Getty Images Entertainment via Getty Images; pages 48/49: CBS Photo Archive / CBS via Getty Images; pages 52/53: Stuart C. Wilson / Getty Images Entertainment via Getty Images; pages 56/57: Handout / Getty Images News via Getty Images

ISBN: 978-1-68021-885-5
eBook: 978-1-64598-209-8

Printed in Malaysia

27 26 25 24 23   2 3 4 5 6

Table of Contents

CHAPTER 1
Science Superstar 4

CHAPTER 2
Early Life 8

CHAPTER 3
Oxford Days 14

CHAPTER 4
Turning Point 18

CHAPTER 5
The Beginning of a Career 22

CHAPTER 6
On the Rise 28

CHAPTER 7
Finding a New Voice 34

CHAPTER 8
Spreading Ideas 40

CHAPTER 9
Pop Scientist 48

CHAPTER 10
Looking Ahead 52

Glossary 58

CHAPTER 1
Science Superstar

He was as famous as a rock star. His book sold ten million copies. Shows like *The Simpsons* and *Star Trek* used him as a character.

His voice was electronic. A computer made it. Some thought it sounded funny. But it let him ask daring questions. What happened before the **universe** began? Can we go back in time? What is real, and what is imaginary?

The work he did was important. It helped solve some of science's greatest puzzles. **Black holes** were one focus. Time travel was another.

His name was Stephen Hawking. There was no question too big for him to ask. He believed all people deserve answers. The secrets of the universe are not just for scientists, he said. They are for everyone to know.

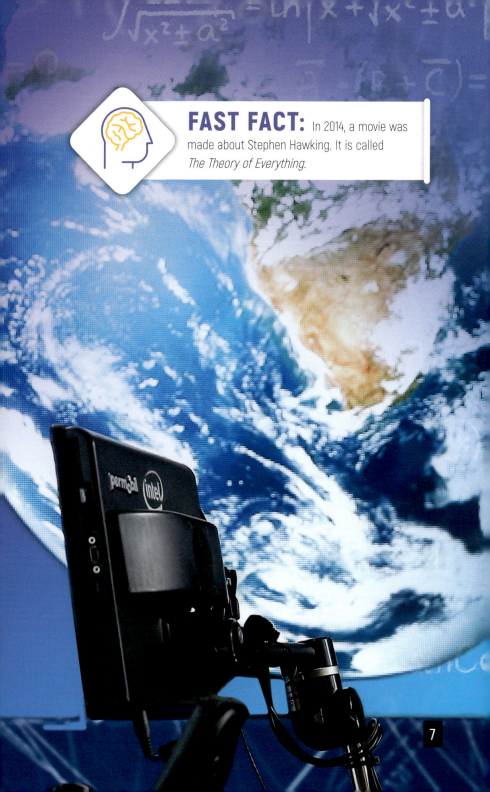

FAST FACT: In 2014, a movie was made about Stephen Hawking. It is called *The Theory of Everything*.

CHAPTER 2

Early Life

Stephen William Hawking was born on January 8, 1942. This was during World War II. His parents lived in London, England. Planes were bombing the city. Hawking's mom left to give birth. She went to Oxford. It was safer there.

BORN TO SHINE

Hawking was proud of his birthday. It was the 300th anniversary of Galileo's death. Galileo was a famous astronomer. He created a powerful telescope that he used to discover Saturn's rings and Jupiter's moons.

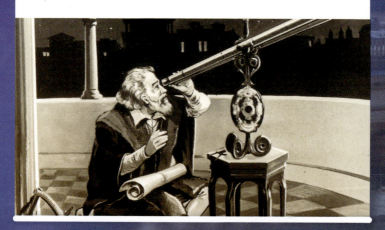

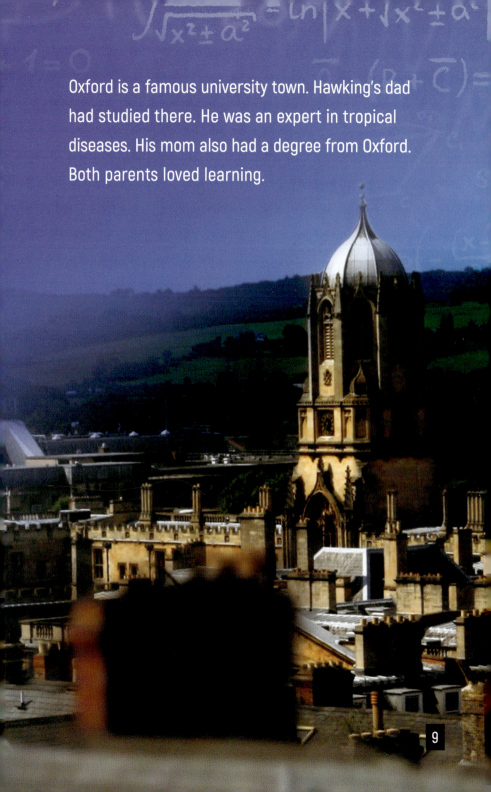

Oxford is a famous university town. Hawking's dad had studied there. He was an expert in tropical diseases. His mom also had a degree from Oxford. Both parents loved learning.

A Curious Family

Stephen was the Hawkings' first child. They had three other children after him. The family lived in a big house. It was just outside London.

Neighbors found them a bit strange. Mr. Hawking kept bees in the basement. He bought an old taxi to use as the family car. The Hawkings made fireworks for fun. Each year, they went camping in a bright green van.

Hawking's parents encouraged him to be curious. Together they visited museums. The family looked at stars in the night sky.

Travel was a big part of their lives too. Hawking's father went on trips to Africa. His mom took the kids to a Spanish island. Once the family spent months in India. They stayed on a houseboat there.

FAST FACT: Stephen and his sister Mary, who loved to climb, used to figure out different ways to get into the family home.

School Struggles

School was tough for Hawking. He did not learn to read until he was eight. His grades were not very good. Teachers said his work was sloppy.

He had other interests, though. One was taking apart model trains. His goal was to find out how they worked. Later, he built model airplanes and boats. This led to an interest in science. Hawking wanted to know what made the world work. How did airplanes fly? Where did electricity come from? What caused **gravity**?

Hawking's dad helped him with math. His dream was for his son to be a doctor. But Hawking's interests were far from Earth. He wanted to know how the whole universe worked.

FAST FACT: Despite his poor grades, Hawking was recognized as a smart child. He built a computer with his friends, and his classmates gave him the nickname "Einstein."

CHAPTER 3

Oxford Days

Hawking was eager to learn. At 17, he applied to Oxford. He got in. It was time to pick an area of study. **Physics** was the clear choice. This would help him answer questions about how the world worked.

In 1959, Hawking began his studies. He was lonely at first. Most students were much older. They had done military service. Hawking felt left out.

To make friends, he joined the Boat Club. This was a racing team. Eight people rowed the boat. Hawking sat at the front. He was the **coxswain**. His job was to steer.

The group became close. They spent a lot of time together. Little studying got done.

After three years, it was time for final exams. Hawking did poorly. He had hoped to graduate with honors. But his grades were a bit low.

Teachers met with Hawking. They debated whether he deserved honors. He had a feeling they did not like him. This gave him an idea. Hawking made them an offer. If they gave him honors, he would leave Oxford. Otherwise he would stay. The teachers gave him honors.

It was time to plan his next steps. One idea was to go to Cambridge. There, he could continue studying science. He also had a backup plan to work in government. To do this, he had to take an exam. Hawking scheduled the test. Then he forgot all about it. That helped settle the matter. He would go to Cambridge.

FAST FACT: Oxford and Cambridge are the two most famous universities in England. Oxford was founded in the year 1096. Cambridge was founded in 1209.

CHAPTER 4

Turning Point

In 1962, Hawking entered Cambridge. He began his research in **cosmology**. The field covers big questions. How did the universe begin? What is it made of? How does it work?

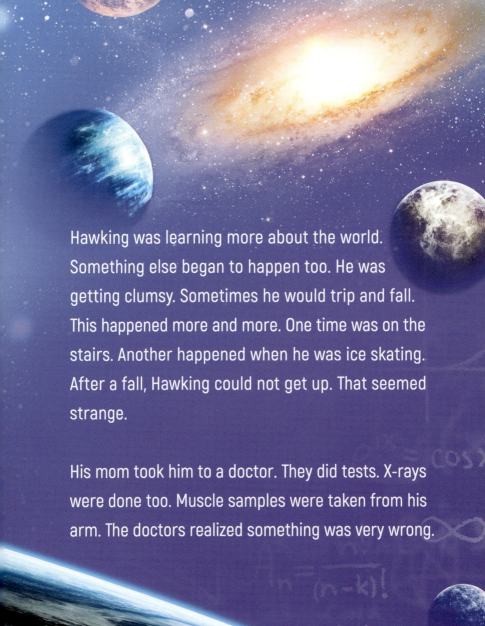

Hawking was learning more about the world. Something else began to happen too. He was getting clumsy. Sometimes he would trip and fall. This happened more and more. One time was on the stairs. Another happened when he was ice skating. After a fall, Hawking could not get up. That seemed strange.

His mom took him to a doctor. They did tests. X-rays were done too. Muscle samples were taken from his arm. The doctors realized something was very wrong.

Diagnosis

Doctors told Hawking the news. His case was unusual. He had a disease. It was called ALS. This attacks the muscles. They stop working over time. People with ALS become **paralyzed**.

His doctors said there was no cure. It would just keep getting worse. Hawking might only have a few years to live. The news filled him with despair.

Then something happened to change his view. There was a young boy in the next bed at the hospital. He died of leukemia. Hawking realized something. Others had it worse than him. At least he was still alive. There was time left.

Hawking thought about his life. What if it was cut short? That meant every minute counted. Each day mattered. Then he made a decision. It was time to do some good while he still could.

FAST FACT: ALS stands for amyotrophic lateral sclerosis. It is also known as Lou Gehrig's disease. Lou Gehrig was a famous baseball player who got the disease in the 1930s.

ALS

ALS causes nerve cells in the brain and spinal cord to break down. The brain loses its ability to control muscles. In time, the muscles weaken and waste away.

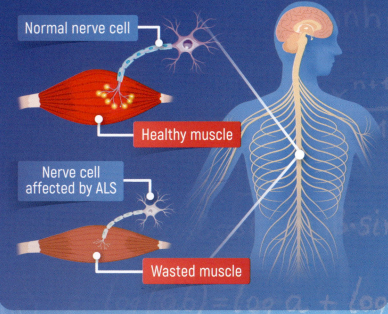

CHAPTER 5

The Beginning of a Career

Hawking went back to school. At first this was hard. He did not know how long he would live. But the feeling faded. Time passed. Life became fun again.

Soon he fell in love with another student. Her name was Jane Wilde. They got engaged. This gave him something to look forward to. The two were married in July of 1965.

Hawking also applied for a research **fellowship**. Jane helped him fill out the forms. His hands were too shaky to write or type.

He got the fellowship. But there was a lot of catching up to do. His math needed work. There were theories to learn. Hawking went to **lectures** and talks. He studied as much as possible. A new determination pushed him forward.

THEORIES

Physicists create theories to explain why events take place. A theory is an idea that can be tested and has evidence to back it up. If enough evidence supports a theory, it becomes widely accepted. For example, centuries ago there were two theories about Earth and the sun. One theory said the sun revolved around Earth. The other stated that Earth revolved around the sun. The invention of the telescope helped astronomers find enough evidence to support the second theory. Only then was it accepted.

Big Ideas

Hawking's advisor was Dennis Sciama. The two studied the Big Bang. This is a theory about how the universe began. Calculations showed the universe started as a tiny point. Suddenly, it exploded. Energy and **matter** burst out. They spread far. Stars and planets formed.

Black holes were also part of Hawking's studies. These begin as stars. Then they collapse in on themselves. All of their **mass** presses into a tiny point at the center. This creates a strong force of gravity. Objects around it are pulled in. Even light cannot escape. That is why black holes appear black.

FAST FACT: The greater an object's mass, the more gravity it exerts on other objects.

Hawking studied the two ideas. A thought struck him. In a black hole, everything disappeared into a tiny point. During the Big Bang, everything exploded out of a tiny point. To Hawking, the Big Bang was like a black hole in reverse.

This was a bold idea. It caught the interest of an **astronomer**. His name was Roger Penrose. The two worked on Hawking's theory. They published a paper. It used ideas from black holes to help explain the Big Bang.

Penrose had discovered that something strange happens inside a black hole. Space and time come to an end. Hawking showed that the reverse might be true of the Big Bang. It may have been the beginning of space and time.

EINSTEIN, SPACE, AND TIME

Both Hawking and Penrose built on the work of Albert Einstein. Einstein lived from 1879 to 1955. He believed space and time were part of a single fabric called "space-time." Space-time becomes so warped inside black holes that it disappears completely. As a result, time does not pass inside a black hole. Hawking believed time also did not occur before the Big Bang.

CHAPTER 6
On the Rise

Hawking's work got attention. He was not afraid to ask big questions. Other scientists noticed. They wanted to meet him. Hawking was invited to universities around the world. He became a rising star.

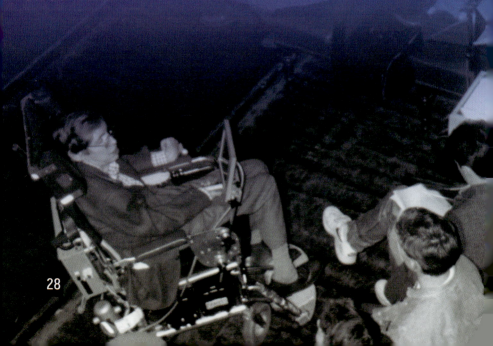

His family was growing too. Jane had their first child in 1967. This was Robert. Lucy was next. Later, they had a son named Timothy.

Unfortunately, Hawking's ALS kept getting worse. Walking became a struggle. It was hard to get around. But the physicist did not want to quit. He began using a wheelchair. Assistants helped him with tasks. The family also moved to a ground-floor apartment. All of these things allowed him to carry on. His work continued. Hawking's best ideas were yet to come.

Mini Black Holes

In 1971, Hawking had a new idea. Black holes did not have to be big. Some could be tiny. He called these mini black holes. They may have formed at the start of the universe.

People thought nothing could escape from a black hole. Hawking thought so too. Then he learned something new. Black holes could shrink. When they did, **radiation** escaped. Now it is called "Hawking radiation." This was an important finding. It revealed more about how the universe works.

FAST FACT: The core of the sun is approximately 15,000,000 degrees Kelvin. You would need to add another 42 zeros to that number to reach the temperature of a mini black hole.

A Theory of Everything

Scientists have long had a dream. It is to find one set of rules to explain the whole universe. They call this a theory of everything. No one has found it yet.

Instead, they have found two different sets of rules. One set covers large objects. Things like people and planets are in this group. The other covers small objects. These are tinier than an atom. The two sets of rules do not agree. This is a problem. It means something is missing from what we know.

Mini black holes may offer an answer. These are very tiny. But they have a huge mass. The rules of both small and large objects should apply to them.

Hawking did calculations. These helped connect the behavior of small and large objects. This was a big step toward finding a theory of everything. Experts still don't have a complete theory for the universe. But Hawking's work on black holes brings them much closer.

GROWING RECOGNITION

Hawking began to receive honors for his work. In 1974, he was elected a Fellow of the Royal Society. This award goes to the most important scientists in the world. In 1979, he was offered a top job at Cambridge. He became the Lucasian Professor of Mathematics. Sir Isaac Newton, who discovered the laws of motion in 1686, once held this post.

CHAPTER 7

Finding a New Voice

Years passed. It was the 1980s. Hawking was still alive. He felt fortunate. But there were new challenges.

The disease moved to his throat. This led to choking fits. His speech was affected. Hawking's voice grew hard to understand. **Interpreters** spoke for him. They repeated his words to others. It helped him communicate.

A Brush with Death

In 1985, Hawking went to Switzerland. There, he visited CERN. This is a nuclear lab. His throat got worse. He came down with **pneumonia**.

Hawking was rushed to the hospital. Doctors thought he might die. They did a **tracheotomy**. It saved his life. But there was a price to pay. He would never be able to talk again.

A Dark Time

The days that followed were difficult. Hawking could not speak. He could not type. All his ideas were trapped inside. It seemed like his career might be over.

Then there was a sliver of hope. Someone held up a card with the alphabet on it. They pointed to letters one by one. Hawking raised an eyebrow. This meant stop. He could spell that way. It let him communicate basic needs. But the process was slow.

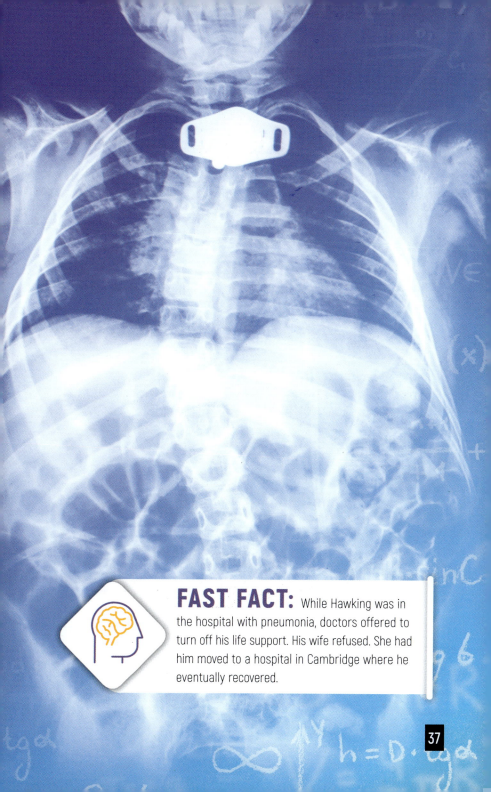

FAST FACT: While Hawking was in the hospital with pneumonia, doctors offered to turn off his life support. His wife refused. She had him moved to a hospital in Cambridge where he eventually recovered.

Equalizer

A **programmer** in California heard what happened to Hawking. His name was Walt Woltosz. He had a program. It was called Equalizer. Woltosz sent it to Hawking.

The program had sets of words. Hawking pressed a switch in his hand. It scrolled through them. He could click on his choice. Next, the words were sent to a speech **synthesizer**. A computer read them aloud. This gave Hawking a voice. Now he could "talk" again.

Hawking communicated this way for years. Then his thumb stopped working. He could no longer click. A new switch had to be made. It was a "cheek switch." Hawking wore special glasses. They had a sensor that picked up motion. Hawking tensed muscles in his cheek. This let him choose words. Thanks to the cheek switch, he could keep talking.

A FAMOUS VOICE

Hawking's electronic voice was created by an engineer at Massachusetts Institute of Technology. The voice was called Perfect Paul. Hawking used this voice for several years. Later, programmers offered him a newer, better voice. But Hawking decided to stay with Perfect Paul. By this time, many people knew him by that voice.

CHAPTER 8

Spreading Ideas

Hawking could only write a few words a minute. Still, he was determined to share his ideas. Many would have given up. He did not.

It took patience. But there was no stopping him. The physicist took it one word at a time. All the words added up. Hawking wrote over ten books. He published paper after paper. His lectures and talks continued.

Reaching Out

Hawking worked with top physicists. But he wanted to reach beyond that. Ordinary people should know about the universe too, he believed. After all, it was their home.

This gave him an idea. He would write a book. It would not be for scientists. Instead, it would be for the public. The book would tell all about the universe. He would start from the beginning of time. Simple language would be used. Anyone could read it.

Publishers thought the book would not sell. Normal people will not care, they said. The ideas are too hard. Few would read it.

Hawking proved them wrong. In 1988, he wrote the book. The title was *A Brief History of Time*. It was an instant best seller. Over ten million copies were sold.

FAST FACT: *A Brief History of Time* spent 147 weeks on the *New York Times* best-seller list and a record-breaking 237 weeks on the *Times of London* best-seller list.

Secrets of the Universe

The book was popular for many reasons. Hawking made difficult ideas easy to understand. He posed big questions. How did the universe start? Where does it end? What is empty space made of? The answers were strange and wonderful.

Hawking showed that space is **warped**. Time can warp too. It passes at different speeds in different places.

The book explored whether aliens could visit. It told where stars come from. Stories were used to bring ideas to life.

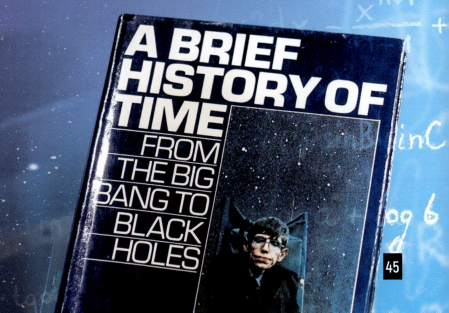

In one story, there are twin brothers. One goes on a trip. He travels at the speed of light. When he comes back, he is still young. But his twin is old.

Another story tells of an astronaut. He visits a black hole. Gravity is stronger at his feet than at his head. This stretches him out like a piece of spaghetti.

Hawking also talked about time travel. A ship takes a shortcut through space. This is called a **wormhole**. It allows the ship to go back in time.

Readers loved these ideas. They wanted to learn more. It was the start of a new trend. Cosmology grew popular. Science became cool. Hawking proved that physics was for everyone.

COSMOS FOR KIDS

Hawking wanted young people to learn about the cosmos too. He and his daughter, Lucy, wrote a book series for kids. It is about a character named George who travels across time and space. The first book was called *George's Secret Key to the Universe*.

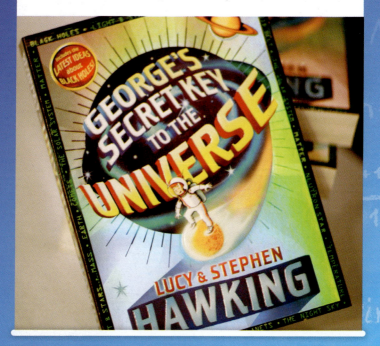

CHAPTER 9

Pop Scientist

Hawking was not just a science fan. He also loved TV. *The Simpsons* was a favorite show. Its creators liked him too. They invited him on the show. Hawking appeared four times. Artists drew him into scenes. In one, he talks with Homer Simpson. They discuss the universe. Homer suggests it might be shaped like a doughnut. Hawking says that is a great idea.

Star Trek also had him on the show. He was on *The Big Bang Theory* too. His voice is part of a *Futurama* video game. It is on two Pink Floyd albums as well.

Funny Man

Hawking was known for his jokes. He loved to laugh. Humor got him through hard times. It also helped him explain complex ideas.

One was parallel universes. His math showed something strange. Ours may not be the only universe. There could be others. Each might be just a little bit different. This was a big idea. It was tough to understand. But Hawking used funny stories to help.

Once he spoke to a crowd. A teen asked a question. She loved the band One Direction. But her favorite singer left the group. How would this affect the cosmos? Hawking told her not to worry. In a parallel universe, he was still with the band. In yet another universe, she was happily married to him. The crowd roared with laughter.

Hawking was also on *Last Week Tonight*. Host John Oliver asked a question. Was there a parallel universe where he was smarter than Hawking? Hawking answered, "Yes. And also a universe where you're funny."

A *Simpsons* producer summed it up. Hawking had "a sense of humor as vast as the universe," he said.

FAST FACT: Hawking came up with a way for a space probe to someday test whether parallel universes really exist.

CHAPTER 10

Looking Ahead

Doctors said Hawking would not live past his 20s. Instead, he lived to see the year 2000. The new century was an exciting time for him. Technology was changing. Possibilities were everywhere. Hawking took part in many projects. He kept learning and growing.

One project was iBrain. This is a device. A band is worn on the head. It picks up thoughts. Hawking worked with the team. He tested it out. Their goal was to help people with ALS.

He also joined Breakthrough Listen. This group has big plans. They look for life in outer space. Someday, tiny ships will go out. These will visit other planets. The group hopes to find new worlds.

Hawking liked to think far ahead. What if something happened to Earth? Having another place to go would be smart. He thought about moving to other planets. People could make homes in outer space.

AI interested him too. This is artificial intelligence. It is when computers act like humans. They could do many jobs. But Hawking saw a risk. He warned people. Be careful. Do not let AI get too smart. It might take over the world.

Honoring a Great Mind

Hawking won many of the top prizes in science. Schools gave him honorary degrees. World leaders honored him too. One was the Queen of England. Another was U.S. President Barack Obama. The Pope also gave him a medal.

Hawking's Awards & Prizes

- **1966** — Adams Prize
- **1975** — Pius XI Medal
- **1975** — Eddington Medal
- **1976** — Hughes Medal
- **1979** — Albert Einstein Medal
- **1988** — Wolf Prize in Physics
- **2006** — Copley Medal
- **2008** — Fonseca Prize
- **2009** — Presidential Medal of Freedom
- **2013** — Breakthrough Prize in Fundamental Physics

Stephen Hawking died on March 14, 2018. He was 76 years old. His life was fuller and grander than anyone could have dreamed.

People remembered his gifts to science. He helped us think bigger. But there was much more. His determination was inspiring. It showed something important. A body may have limits. The mind can still do great things. Hawking's mind traveled to the edges of the universe. He brought back answers to some of our toughest questions.

Hawking was guided by a sense of purpose. "My goal is simple," he said. "It is a complete understanding of the universe." His work may help us get there.

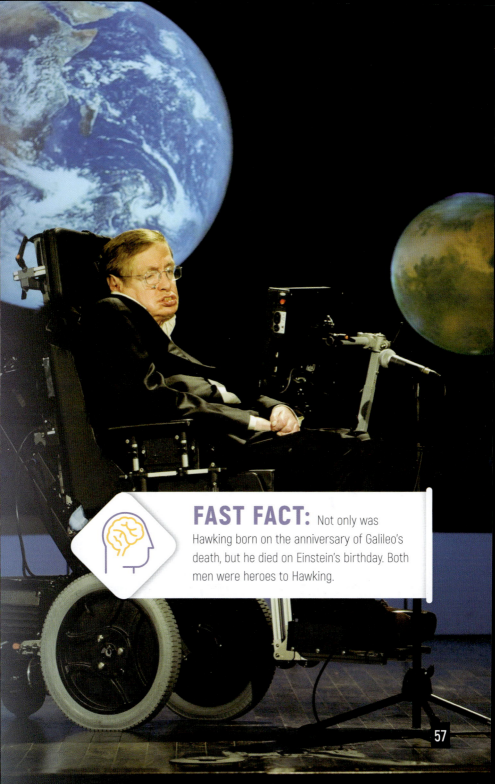

FAST FACT: Not only was Hawking born on the anniversary of Galileo's death, but he died on Einstein's birthday. Both men were heroes to Hawking.

Glossary

astronomer: a person who studies the planets, stars, and space

black hole: an area in space where the force of gravity sucks everything in

cosmology: the study of the universe and how it began

coxswain: a person who steers a boat

fellowship: money awarded to support a student's research

gravity: the force of attraction between two objects; the force that pulls things toward the center of a moon, planet, or black hole

interpreter: a person who translates speech so people can understand each other

lecture: a talk given to teach something

mass: the amount of matter in an object

matter: any substance that takes up space

paralyzed: unable to move or feel one's body

physics: the branch of science that deals with matter and energy

pneumonia: a disease that affects the lungs

programmer: a person who writes software code

radiation: an invisible energy given off by an object

synthesizer: a machine that makes sounds electronically

tracheotomy: a medical procedure in which a hole is cut into the windpipe to allow a person to breathe

universe: everything that exists in space

warped: bent or twisted into an unusual shape

wormhole: a hole or passageway in space that some think may connect two places that are very far apart

TAKE A LOOK INSIDE

DROIDS AND ROBOTS

CHAPTER 1

Born in Fiction

A metal arm bends and twists. It welds a car door. A big cat races across a field. This is not like other cats, though. It is made of metal and wire. A woman greets people at a store. Her head is plastic.

These are all robots. Bots is another name. Bots are machines that do tasks on their own. They have been around for a long time. Today's robots are very high tech. Most are run by computers.

Answers

Bots do help people in many ways. Job loss is real, though. What can be done? One answer is schools. There are jobs to fill now. More will come in the future. The tasks have just changed. Robots need to be built. They need repair. All must have software. These jobs take special skills. Math is key. Science is too. Many say schools need to focus more on these subjects.

Some experts point to history. New tech waves result in job loss. This happened in the 1800s. Then came computers in the 1970s. Jobs were lost again, but that did not last. New jobs were created. Many jobs people never predicted. A future with robots may be the same.

Likelihood of Jobs Going to Robots

PREDICTABLE PHYSICAL WORK

78% Routine jobs, like working in an assembly line, preparing food, and packing boxes are more likely to go to robots.

UNPREDICTABLE PHYSICAL WORK

25% Jobs where there is more change in tasks, such as construction and forestry are less likely to go to robots.

CHAPTER 10
Wave of the Future

Robots will get smarter. They will need less human control. People will depend on them more. Androids will even go to Mars.

Robonauts

Robots are in outer space now. They will play a key role in the future. NASA is the U.S. space agency. A team there is making robonauts. These are robots that are made to work in space. One is called R2. It works on the U.S. space station. R2 does work that is too risky for humans.

Today, there are seven robots on Mars. They take photos and collect samples. NASA plans to send androids there too. The R5 is being tested now. It is six feet tall and weighs 290 pounds. A group of them will go ahead of people. They will set up a station. All will then work together with humans.

WHITE LIGHTNING BOOKS® NONFICTION

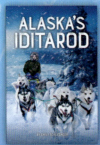
9781680218831

9781680217551

9781680216387

9781680216400

9781680217377

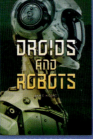
9781680216394

9781680217391

9781680216912

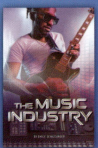
9781680219135

9781680218848

9781680217384

9781680218855

9781680219111

9781680219128

9781680217414

9781680217407

MORE TITLES COMING SOON
SDLBACK.COM/WHITE-LIGHTNING-BOOKS